A Day in the Life of Children Around the World

A Day in the Life of Children Around the World

A Collection of Short Stories

Kathy Kirk

Writers Club Press
Bloomington

A Day in the Life of Children Around the World
A Collection of Short Stories

Writers Club Press
an imprint of iUniverse, Inc.

iUniverse books may be ordered through booksellers or by contacting:

iUniverse
1663 Liberty Drive
Bloomington, IN 47403
www.iuniverse.com
1-800-Authors (1-800-288-4677)

ISBN: 978-0-595-15542-2 (sc)

Printed in the United States of America

iUniverse rev. date: 01/27/2011

This book is dedicated to my family, Laurie, Eldon, Jim, Warren and Jeanette, for their encouragement as I sought to understand the people of many different cultures.

CONTENTS

Learn as much as you can
about all of the
countries in the world

INTRODUCTION

It's time to take a trip around the world! We will be visiting the children of other countries. First, we will spend a day with Ana in a country called Costa Rica in Latin America. Then, we will travel across the Atlantic Ocean to spend a day with Celine in a country called France in Europe. We'll then be off to India, in the Far East, to visit with Rajiv. Our last stop will be the small country of Japan in Asia to visit Miwa.

Enjoy your travels! Learn as much as you can about the children of the world!

A Day in the Life of Ana in Costa Rica-1

Hola! My name is Ana Viquez and I live in a town called Heredia in the country of Costa Rica! Today, you're going to follow me around so I can teach you about my country, my customs, and a little about the language we speak, Spanish.

But first, I'll show you where Costa Rica is. Costa Rica is a small country near the Equator, south of Mexico but north of South America. My region is known as Central America and my country neighbors the countries of Nicaragua and Panama. Since we are so far south, our summers are from November–January! Can you imagine celebrating Christmas in the summertime?

My country is known for its friendly, peaceful people, rainforests, no army or navy, a love for our land and animals, and of course, our coffee and bananas. The people here, called Ticos, have great pride in our country. My country is one of the most beautiful in the world. We have rainforests, cloud forests, volcanoes, sugarcane fields, banana farms, and jungles. We have many beautiful animals here such as toucans, monkeys, and butterflies.

Please come join me in my house. When I wake up, I go right to the table to have breakfast with my family. My mom, "madre", fixes us bread with a sugary white sauce. I have three brothers, "hermanos", and one sister, "hermana". Families are very important in Costa Rica, and children get lots of attention! All of my relatives live in my small town and come over to our home often.

Now you can come with me to my school. I go to a Catholic school. Many of the people in Spain are very religious. We are mostly Catholic because our ancestors were from Spain. They arrived here in the 1500's and we did not get our independence until 1821. They named my country Costa Rica which means "rich coast" in Spanish.

Holidays are very important in my country and there are always big celebrations with parades. The people dress is beautiful Costa Rican costumes with lots of colors.

I'd like to introduce you to my teacher, Señora Rosa. She is a wonderful teacher! And here are some of my friends, Paco, Juan, Maria, and Katia. We learn the same subjects in school as you do. We have an excellent education system in Costa Rica. More people can read and write in my country than any other in Latin America.

We take long lunch breaks so we can go home and eat lunch with our family! Let's go home for lunch now! Oh look, my mom has cooked a typical dish of Costa Rica called Gallos pintos. It is rice, beans, an egg, and tortillas. It is delicious, or in Spanish we say "muy rico".

Oh, look, it's time for recess at school. Soccer is a very popular sport throughout Latin America, and we call it "futbol" here. Let's play!

Now it is time for music lessons. In Costa Rica, our music is a mix of African and Spanish culture. Dancing is very popular here, and our most popular dance styles are called Merengue and Salsa. Can you hear the Latin guitar in this song and the bongo drum? It has a happy beat, and it's hard not to dance when you hear our music.

Now that school is out, let's go back to my house and play with my toys. I bet I have a lot of the same toys as you because toys from the United States are very popular! In a little while, we will take our afternoon "siesta" or rest. Even the adults take rests in the afternoons and some of the stores even close for a few hours.

Can you hear my mom? She is saying "Comecita". In Costa Rica, we use "-ita" at the end of a lot of our words because it sounds very friendly. She is telling us that it's time to eat. We eat our big meal during lunchtime, since lunch is the time to spend a lot of time talking with family.

Just for your visit, my mom has made tamales. It is a traditional Costa Rican meal, which means people have eaten this dish for a long time. It took her two days to prepare and she invited all of her relatives to our home. We always have tamales for Christmas, too. Now what do you say when you really like what you're eating? Yes, "muy rico".

Oh look, my cousins, aunt, uncles, and grandparents have come to visit us tonight. We always have a wonderful time joking and telling stories. My grandparents have brought us some really good sweets!

It is now time for us to go to sleep. I always kneel before my bed and say a prayer before I go to sleep. In Spanish, we start our prayers with "Querido Dios" which means "Dear God".

I hope that what you've learned about my country–the people, the customs, the language–will make you want to learn more. Please share what you've learned with your friends and family so they will want to come visit me.

In Costa Rica, giving gifts to others is very important. Since I've really enjoyed having you, I've gotten you something so you will always remember your visit. It is a miniature oxen cart! Many years ago, these carts were used to carry coffee from the country into town. Beautiful designs are painted on the carts, which make these gifts very popular.

I want to leave you with a phrase that the Costa Ricans are known for and a motto many people live their life around: "Todo Bien". It means "everything is great". In other words, don't let things get you down–just live life to the fullest and be happy."

Have a great trip back home, mi amigo (my friend). Come back to visit soon. Adios (Bye)!

A Day in the Life
of Celine in France-2

"Bonjour" (Good Day)! My name is Celine Dechaine and I live in a town near Paris, the capital of the country of France! Today, you're going to follow me around so I can teach you about my country, my customs, and a little about the language we speak, French.

But first, I'll show you where France is. France is in a region called Europe just across the Atlantic Ocean, east of America. France is located in Western Europe, and borders eight countries including Spain, Italy, Switzerland, Germany, and is across the English Channel from England. France is the largest country in size, in Western Europe.

A long time ago, the people who lived in France were called Gauls and were related to people from Ireland and Wales. Later, before the time of Christ, France was conquered by Julius Caesar and the Romans.

My country is known for its rich culture. We also have diverse regions throughout the country, such as our mountains, called the Alps, our beach towns in the south on the Mediterranean sea, our rivers such as the Rhine, and our old castles and palaces such as the palace of King Louis XIV.

We are very strong in the arts such as painting, writing and music. In France, we always make the time to enjoy the good things in life such as art, food, and wine.

Please, come join me in my house. Most people in France live in apartments in the city. When I wake up, I have breakfast with my family. We have a simple breakfast with fresh bread, such as a croissant, and my parents have coffee.

As I get ready for school, I'd like to explain why we're known around the world for our unique fashion. We are very artistic, have great taste, and a certain elegance to our style. How do you like my beret and scarf?

Now you can come with me to my school. I go to a Catholic school. Most of the people in France are Roman Catholic.

School is very important in France. Our teacher teaches us about our castles, our mountains, and our monuments. We spend a lot of time learning about history and the arts. I love to read plays and poems! Our school system has changed a lot so that we learn about subjects like history and science and also modern subjects which will allow us to have good careers.

In France, we learn an ancient language called Latin, which was used in the creation of our language, French. French is known for being a romantic language. Now, I will teach you how to say, "I love you" in French: "Je t'aime".

Today we are learning about the famous artists of France. French artists have been the leaders in world art for many years. There are many famous periods of art history in France, such as the Renaissance in the 1400-1500's and Impressionism in the 1800-1900's.

Tomorrow, we will learn about a famous leader in France's history, Napoleon Bonaparte. Napoleon was a short man with tall ambitions. Napoleon made France the world leader in the early 1800's, when he conquered most of Europe.

Now that school is out, let's go back to my house so I can show you my pictures of the French countryside. Our family also has a home in the country, like many families in France. The country style of living is very important here. Look at my pictures of the wheat and grape crops!

France has more farms than any other country in Western Europe. One third of our country is crops. Do you know how we make wine? We make it from grapes. French wine is the best wine in the world.

It is time for dinner now! Great food is very important in France. We are famous for our breads, rich sauces, and desserts. The dinner my mother has cooked has five courses which means we'll be eating for awhile! In France, we always say "Bon Appetit" before our meal which means, "Enjoy your Meal!"

Tomorrow is an important day for us. It is our Independence Day, just like the United States' Independence Day, called the 4th of July. In France, it is called Bastille Day and it is on July 14. It is the day the people of Paris captured a prison during the Revolution in 1780.

In a few weeks, we will take our summer vacation for five weeks, like everyone in France. I look forward to it every year. We always go to the beach in the south, which we call the Riviera.

I hope that what you've learned about my country–the people, the customs–will make you want to learn more. Please share what you've learned with your friends and family so they, too, will want to come visit me.

Since I've really enjoyed having you here, I've gotten you something so you will always remember your visit. It is a basket of baguettes, a famous bread of France, baked at the small bakery down the street.

I want to leave you with a famous French saying: "France is not only a land, a people, and a state–it is a spirit". It is the spirit of France that has given us our power for many years. I hope you have gotten to understand a little about our French spirit.

Have a great trip back home, "mon ami" (my friend). Come back soon to visit! "Au Revoir" (Goodbye)!!

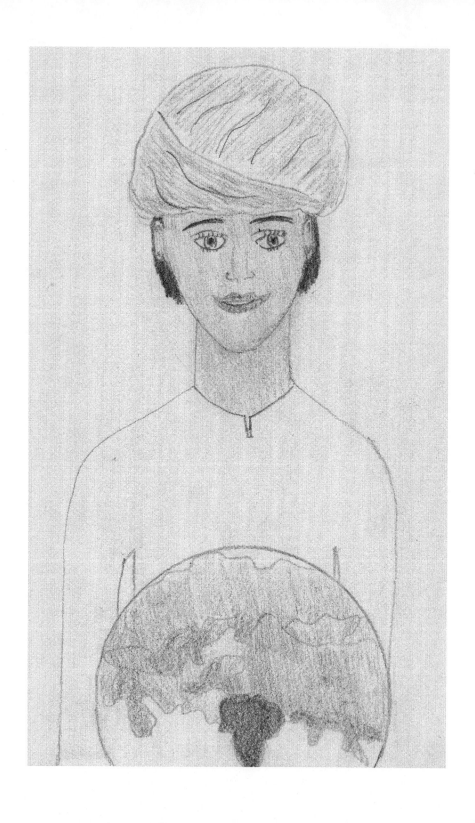

A Day in the Life
of Rajiv in India-3

नमस्ते

This is "Hello" in my language, Hindi. It is pronounced Nah-may-stay! My name is Rajiv Sinha and I live in a small village of less than 1,000 people, near the capital of New Delhi, in the country of India! Today, you're going to follow me around so I can teach you about my country, my customs, and a little about the language we speak.

But first, I'll show you where India is. India is a large country shaped like a pear in a region to the East called Asia. My country neighbors China. We have the second largest number of people of all of the countries in the world.

We are so far away from the United States, that our time is very different. When it is 3:00 in the afternoon in the West Coast of the US, it is 5:00 in the morning in India!

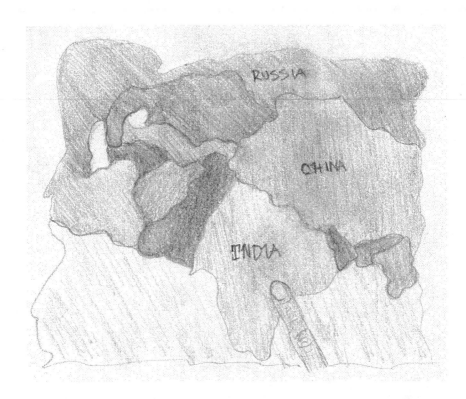

My country is very old and is known for its ancient customs, beautiful cloths, and many differences among our people. India was well known in ancient times for its richness in things like jewels, rugs, silks and spices. Christopher Columbus was looking for an easier way to India when he discovered America.

Please, come join me in my house. Many of the people in India live in small villages like we do. Our homes are made of mud and straw. I help my family out on the farm, and when we come home from school, we will go to the market and help my family sell our farm products!

We have a special type of clothing in India, and we love bright colors. I am wearing a dhoti as clothing and a turban as a hat. My mother is wearing something called a sari, which is a straight piece of cloth wrapped around the body as a long dress. My mother is also wearing a kumkum on the middle of her forehead. This dot is a mark of beauty, and many women wear this mark.

Now you can come with me to my school. I will only go to school until I finish sixth grade. Like many children in India, I will then help my parents on the farm.

Today we are learning about a famous leader in my country, Gandhi. Our country was ruled by England, until Gandhi led millions of us to make a change. We showed England that we wanted to be a country all by ourselves, in a quiet way. We became independent in 1947.

My classroom is filled with pictures of the animals of India. The country has a lot of different types of land—desert, jungles, rainforests, and the tallest mountains in the world, called the Himalayas. So, we have lots of animals like rhinoceroses, elephants, tigers, leopards, and even camels!

On our way back to my house, we pass a temple, which is where I go to worship. My religion is called Hindu. We have many religions in India as well as many languages. People in my country speak 16 different languages, and Hindi is the national language.

Now that we are home, we should help my family sell fruit at the market. See, I carry fruit in a woven basket. It's easy to balance on my head! The market is very crowded, and my country is one of the most overcrowded countries in the world. We have a poor standard of living compared to many countries, but are working hard to improve it.

Now that it is time for dinner, we will get to taste my mother's excellent cooking. In India, bread, rice, vegetables, and pepper seasoning is a common meal. We do not eat meat because of religious beliefs. My mother has prepared a typical dish called rice and dal. Curry sauce is one of my favorites. It is very spicy! Mmmmmm.

Now it's time for us to go to sleep. I hope that what you've learned about my country—its people and customs—makes you want to learn more. Please share what you've learned with your friends and family so they will want to come visit me.

Since I've really enjoyed having you here, I've gotten you something so you will remember your visit. It is a pot of our special, spicy sauce. Do you remember what it's called? Curry!

Before you leave, I will bow to the ground and bless you with a Hindi prayer as I wish the best for you and your trip back home. We always bow to the ground like this when we say prayers.

H ave a great trip back home! Come back soon to visit! "Subha raatri" (Good Night)!!

A Day in the Life
of Miwa in Japan-4

日本語

"Nihongo" means "Hello" in Japanese and this is how it is written. My name is Miwa Sugi and I live in the capital city, Tokyo, in the country of Japan! Today, you're going to follow me around so I can teach you about my country and its customs.

But first, I'll show you where Japan is. Japan is a small country made up of thousands of islands in a region to the East called Asia. Most people live on one of four main islands. We are near China, Korea, and other Eastern Islands. People have lived in Japan for over 30,000 years!

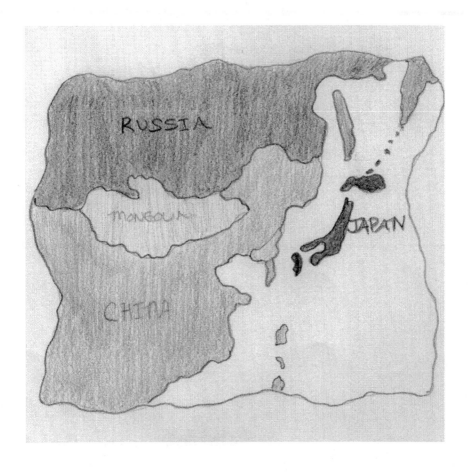

My country is very rugged, so there is not a lot of land for big cities. Most of the people live in big cities, like Tokyo, the biggest city. Did you know we have more than 60 active volcanoes in Japan? We also have a lot of earthquakes.

My country is very old and is known for its art customs, religion, politeness, and the way we do business. Harmony is very important in my country. We are also known for mixing aspects of both the eastern and western worlds. For example, you can be walking down the street and see a baseball game on one corner, and an ancient Japanese dance on the other

We live very well here in Japan and have world famous businesses which make important products such as televisions, computers and cars.

Please come join me in my house. We live in small homes here built from light materials. Many of us don't have central heating, and we like to sit on straw mats. I sleep on a bed called a futon. We have a simple style of living here.

Here in Japan, families are very important and the tie between mothers and children are very close. My father spends a lot of time working. My mother spends a lot of time teaching me new things and helping me with my homework.

Now you can come with me to my school. We will walk to school with a group of children. In Japan, groups are very important. We are very loyal to our groups, and it is an important way of life.

Here we are at school! Education is very important in Japan. We even go to school on Saturdays and I spend a lot of time doing homework. We take a lot of hard tests in order to go to new levels in school. The college I get accepted into is very important to my family.

Today we will learn about poetry. Poetry is very important in Japan. We are learning about a type of poem called Haiku which has 17 syllables. My teacher is reading us a Haiku poem, written by Basho:

An ancient pond.
A frog jumps in.
The sound of water.

My language, Japanese, is very different than English because it is written in symbols. There are 1850 characters in our everyday reading language, called Kanji. Each character means a complete word or syllable. Here is the character for Friend:

友達

On our way back to my house, we pass a temple, which is where I go to worship. See the large tile roof, the beautiful edges, and the wood frame? My religion is called Buddhism.

We have many religions in Japan. Most people are Buddhists, but our native religion is called Shinto. If you walk by a big ceremony in Japan, that is probably a Shinto ceremony.

Now that we are home, I would like to tell you about our arts which are very important. Flower arranging, ceramics, ivory carving, silk weaving and embroidery are all popular. My mother will show you a traditional art–the tea ceremony. Look how pretty the pottery is!

On my backyard, we have a small garden. Gardens with tiny landscapes are very popular in Japan. We have planted things that look like mountains, forests and lakes on our little patio.

Now that it is time for dinner, we will get to taste my mother's excellent cooking. In Japan, we eat mostly rice and fish, along with a cup of tea. We do not eat meat because of religious beliefs.

My father would like to explain our formal culture to you as we eat dinner. Politeness is very important in Japan. We have thousands of rules about how to be polite to other people. One example is that we show our respect to people by bowing. The more important the person, the lower and longer the bow is. Let me show you how it is done!

Since I've really enjoyed having you here, I've gotten you something so you will remember your visit. It is a wood-block print which is a popular type of artwork. In Japan, we like to use bright colors and detailed designs. I hope you like it!

I want to leave you with a Japanese proverb that helps explain our culture: "Makeru ga kachi", which means "To lose is to win".

Have a great trip back home! Come back soon to visit! "Sayounara (Bye)!"

Epilogue

M ay our children live in a world with deep cultural understanding, everywhere.

A portion of the proceeds from this book will be donated to UNICEF.

About the Author

The author has traveled extensively throughout Latin America, Europe, and the Caribbean. She has lived in Toulouse, France, London, England, and San Jose, Costa Rica. The people she has met through these experiences have had the greatest impact on her life. She currently resides in San Diego, California where she works in business. She also has a passion for children, environmentalism, and studying the languages, music, and arts of different cultures.

Please share your comments and suggestions at kkirkendall@hotmail.com. This is the first in the series of books, Culture 4 Kids. It is the author's hope that children have a good understanding of other cultures, and thus live in a harmonious world with appreciation and love of the world's differences.

Made in the USA
Lexington, KY
07 February 2012